LAKE CLASSICS

*Great American
Short Stories II*

Frank R. STOCKTON

Stories retold by Prescott Hill
Illustrated by James McConnell

LAKE EDUCATION
Belmont, California

LAKE CLASSICS

Great American Short Stories I
Washington Irving, Nathaniel Hawthorne, Mark Twain, Bret Harte, Edgar Allan Poe, Kate Chopin, Willa Cather, Sarah Orne Jewett, Sherwood Anderson, Charles W. Chesnutt

Great American Short Stories II
Herman Melville, Stephen Crane, Ambrose Bierce, Jack London, Edith Wharton, Charlotte Perkins Gilman, Frank R. Stockton, Hamlin Garland, O. Henry, Richard Harding Davis

Great British and Irish Short Stories
Arthur Conan Doyle, Saki (H. H. Munro), Rudyard Kipling, Katherine Mansfield, Thomas Hardy, E. M. Forster, Robert Louis Stevenson, H. G. Wells, John Galsworthy, James Joyce

Great Short Stories from Around the World
Guy de Maupassant, Anton Chekhov, Leo Tolstoy, Selma Lagerlöf, Alphonse Daudet, Mori Ogwai, Leopoldo Alas, Rabindranath Tagore, Fyodor Dostoevsky, Honoré de Balzac

Cover and Text Designer: Diann Abbott

Copyright © 1994 by Lake Education, a division of Lake Publishing Company, 500 Harbor Blvd., Belmont, CA 94002. All rights reserved. No part of this book may be reproduced by any means, transmitted, or translated into a machine language without written permission from the publisher.

Library of Congress Catalog Number: 94-075028
ISBN 1-56103-020-1
Printed in the United States of America
1 9 8 7 6 5 4 3 2

CONTENTS

Introduction 5
About the Author 7

The Lady or the Tiger? 9
The Griffin and the Minor Canon 23
The Widow's Cruise 47
A Piece of Red Calico 67

Thinking About the Stories 78

🌿 Lake Classic Short Stories 🌿

"The universe is made of stories, not atoms."
—Muriel Rukeyser

"The story's about you."
—Horace

Everyone loves a good story. It is hard to think of a friendlier introduction to classic literature. For one thing, short stories are *short*—quick to get into and easy to finish. Of all the literary forms, the short story is the least intimidating and the most approachable.

Great literature is an important part of our human heritage. In the belief that this heritage belongs to everyone, *Lake Classic Short Stories* are adapted for today's readers. Lengthy sentences and paragraphs are shortened. Archaic words are replaced. Modern punctuation and spellings are used. Many of the longer stories are abridged. In all the stories, painstaking care has been taken to preserve the author's unique voice.

Lake Classic Short Stories have something for everyone. The hundreds of stories in the collection cover a broad terrain of themes, story types, and styles. Literary merit was a deciding factor in story selection. But no story was included unless it was as enjoyable as it was instructive. And special priority was given to stories that shine light on the human condition.

Each book in the *Lake Classic Short Stories* is devoted to the work of a single author. Little-known stories of merit are included with famous old favorites. Taken as a whole, the collected authors and stories make up a rich and diverse sampler of the story-teller's art.

Lake Classic Short Stories guarantee a great reading experience. Readers who look for common interests, concerns, and experiences are sure to find them. Readers who bring their own gifts of perception and appreciation to the stories will be doubly rewarded.

🌱 Frank R. Stockton 🌿
(1834–1902)

About the Author

Frank R. Stockton was born in Philadelphia. His family had settled in America in the 17th century. One of his ancestors was a signer of the Declaration of Independence.

Stockton started his career as a newspaper reporter in Philadelphia and New York. Then he began writing humorous pieces for *Vanity Fair* magazine. Later he joined the staff of *Scribner's Magazine* and then went to *St. Nicholas*, a children's magazine.

His first book, *Rudder Grange* (1879), was very popular. It was the story of two newlyweds who live in an abandoned canal boat.

Stockton was said to be a sweet-tempered man, even though his health was always poor. His many friends appreciated his wit and good humor. Like many funny men, he wrote slowly and painfully.

The Griffin and the Minor Canon is considered to be one of Stockton's finest stories. But it was another story that made him famous. *The Lady or the Tiger?* was first published in 1882. Six years later, an operetta was based on it.

The success of this one story made it possible for Stockton to write full-time. Soon he began to write more for adults than for children. Yet there was always a close connection between his stories for children and those for adults. A sense of humor and a love of the fanciful are present in both.

Stockton wrote one of the first science fiction stories, "A Tale of Negative Gravity." It appeared in *Century Magazine* in December 1884.

Do you enjoy reading about characters who have unique and sometimes funny problems? If so, you'll like Frank Stockton.

The Lady or the Tiger?

Some decisions are almost impossible to make. This is one of the world's most famous stories about mixed motives. For 100 years, readers have been puzzled by its outcome.

WHAT IF HER LOVER PICKED THE WRONG DOOR? COULD SHE STAND SUCH A SIGHT?

The Lady or the Tiger?

Long ago there lived a king who had strange ideas for his time. Most people who have strange ideas can do nothing about them. But it must be remembered that he was a king. In his country he could do just as he pleased.

One thing he wanted was to be fair to his people—all of them. He even wanted to be fair to people accused of crimes. He wanted them to have trials to decide if they were guilty or not. In most other places, that was decided by juries and judges. But this king thought he had a better idea. He had thought about it for a long time. He did not seek advice from his advisors. He did not ask help from his many helpers. He came up with the idea all by himself. That was the kind of king he was.

His plan was really quite simple. Those accused of crimes would go to the arena. The king's arena was a circle of sand with a high wall all around it. Above the wall were rows of seats for the king's people. Of course there was also a special place where the king sat. It was a lot fancier than the other seats.

The arena was not very large. It might take a man only 30 steps to walk across it. If he ran, a man might get across it in 20 steps. But that was not likely. Most men who had to run in the arena never got that far.

The wall around the arena was 12 feet high. It was smooth as ice. Once a man was in the arena, he could not climb out. The only way a man could get out was the same way he got in. That was through the *one* door on the east side. On the west side were *two* doors. All three doors were part of the king's idea for judging people.

Here is how the idea worked: When a man was accused of a crime, he was sent to the arena. He would step through the door on the east side and out onto the sand. There he would be judged. The strange part was—it was he himself who would do the judging.

How could that be? That is a good question. The answer is simple, once you know about the two doors on the west side. Both of those doors *looked* the same. They were the same size and the same color. There was no way in the world to tell one from the other.

The man in the arena would have to choose which one to open. It could be either door. His choice was his own decision. What could be more fair than that? Even the king could not tell him which door to pick. You might say the accused man would become his own judge when he made his choice.

Behind one of the doors would be a hungry tiger. It would be the wildest beast the king's men could find. Behind the other would be a beautiful lady.

If the man opened the first door, the hungry tiger would come out. As you might guess, the tiger would not be hungry for long. As soon as the tiger killed the man, a bell would ring. The people in the crowd would shed tears. (They were paid by the king to do so!) They would tell each other what a sad day it was. They would say what a shame it was that the poor man was so young—or so old. Then they would all go home.

No one could be blamed except the man himself. After all—he was the one who picked the door. In a sense, he had judged himself guilty.

But what if the man picked the other door? That was a whole different story. That would prove he was *not* guilty.

The people in the audience were always happy when that happened. They would laugh and shout and clap their hands. The beautiful lady would be the man's new bride. This would happen even if he wanted to marry someone else. It would happen even if he already had a wife and family! He would *have* to marry the lady behind the door. It was his reward—whether he liked it or not. There was no time to think it over. The wedding took place then and there.

The king thought his idea was very fair. The people thought so too. To them, the trials in the arena were real treats. Part of the fun was in not knowing what would happen. Maybe it would turn out to be a scary, bloody event! But then, maybe it would be a happy time that ended with a lovely wedding.

Whatever happened in the arena, it was always interesting.

The king had a beautiful daughter named Helen. He loved her very much. And of course he wanted the best of everything for her. Most of all, he wanted her to marry a rich man and live happily ever after.

But Helen had a different idea. She was in love with a young man named Jason. He had little money, but that did not bother her. Jason was handsome, kind, and very sweet. She spent as much time with him as she could. She wanted to marry him. And she was used to getting what she wanted.

But this time was different.

Sad to say, the king was not pleased with Jason. He was so upset, he had Jason thrown in jail. If that seems harsh—think of the king's feelings. He wanted his daughter to be happy. But how could she be happy if she married a poor man? The king thought he knew his daughter better than she knew herself. He knew that she was used to the best of everything. A poor man could not possibly give her that.

The king thought that the young man was making trouble. And in his country, that was a crime. But he wanted to be fair. He saw that there needed to be a trial. Was Jason guilty of a crime? That could only be decided in the arena.

When a date was set for the trial, all the people were told about it. Then the king's men set to work.

First they found a very fierce tiger. He was the biggest and meanest they had ever seen. His teeth were long, yellow, and sharp as razors. His roar made buildings shake.

Then they found the perfect lady. She was the most beautiful woman in the country. Her hair was the color of gold. Her lips were as red as rubies. Her voice was as sweet as a bird's song. Her eyes were as blue as the sky. Her name was Ramona.

Everything was ready. At last it was time for the trial. People came from all over to see what would happen in the arena. It was the biggest event of the year. Never before had there had been such a trial. But never before had a poor man dared to love the king's daughter!

The king sat in his special seat. His daughter sat right next to him. Her chair was almost as fancy as the king's. When all was ready, the signal was given.

Then the east door opened, and Jason stepped into the arena. All the people began to cheer and clap their hands. Many had never seen such a handsome young man before.

Jason started across the arena, then stopped. He turned and bowed to the king. But he kept his eyes on Helen. You might think Helen would have stayed away. After all, what if her lover picked the wrong door? Could she stand such a sight?

She did not think she would have to. In fact, she felt she knew which door Jason would pick. That was because she herself knew what was behind each door. It had cost her a lot of money to find out. But she thought it was worth it. She knew where the tiger was, and she knew where the lady was. She also knew that the lady was Ramona.

Helen had known Ramona for a long time. But you could not say that they were old friends. In fact, Helen hated Ramona. That was not just because Ramona was more beautiful than she. There was another, more important reason. Helen had seen the way Ramona looked at Jason. She knew what that look meant. Ramona was in love with Jason!

As Jason looked up at Helen, their eyes met. Lovers often find ways to talk to each other without using words. That was true for Jason and Helen. As he looked into her eyes, he could almost read her thoughts. He saw at once that she knew the secret. She already knew which door hid the tiger and which hid the lady. It did not surprise him. He knew how smart she was. He had guessed she would find a way to learn the secret.

As he looked at her, Jason tipped his head to one side. His look seemed to ask the question: "Which door?" He could tell that she knew what he meant.

Helen raised one finger and pointed to the door on the right. No one but Jason saw her do it. The king and all the other people had their eyes on the young man.

Jason turned and walked across the arena. Every heart stopped beating. Every breath was held tight. Without stopping, he went to the door on the right and opened it.

Now the point of the story is this: Did the tiger come out, or did the lady?

The more you ask the question, the harder it is to answer. You have to think about what Helen was thinking. She would lose her lover either way. The question was: Should Ramona get him?

Helen had thought and thought about which door Jason would pick. She had imagined the tiger leaping out and attacking the young man. Oh! What an awful sight that would be!

She had also thought about his opening the other door. That might be even worse. Would he smile as Ramona stepped toward him? Would all the people cheer as Jason and Ramona kissed? Would there be a big, happy wedding party?

These thoughts filled Helen's heart with jealousy. If Ramona and Jason lived happily ever after—she would be sad ever after. Maybe it would be best if the tiger got her lover. Then it would be all over with quickly. And yet, the thought of Jason's death seemed awful to her.

It had taken just a moment for her to point to the door on the right. But it was not a quick decision. She had been thinking it over for days.

It is not easy to say what she decided. It is certain that I am not the person who can best answer that. So, I leave it all up to you.

Which came out of the opened door— the lady or the tiger?

The Griffin and the Minor Canon

Suppose that a strange and frightening beast came to visit your town. Who would you call for help? Read on to see what happens when a gentle young priest tries to rescue the town.

It was a statue of a griffin—a strange animal that was part bird and part lion. It was not a pretty sight.

The Griffin and the Minor Canon

Long ago in a town far away there stood a grand old church. Above the front door of the church was a stone carving. It was a statue of a griffin—a strange animal that was part bird and part lion. It was not a pretty sight.

The griffin had a large head with a big sharp beak. It had great wings with hooks on the ends of them. It had the paws of a lion, with savage claws. And it also had a long tail with a barbed point on its tip.

The man who carved the griffin must have been happy with his work. All over the church he had also carved many little griffins just like the big one. Of course, there were other strange animals carved there, too. But none were so strange and terrible as the big griffin and the little ones.

In the wild woods far from town, there was something even stranger. A *real* griffin lived there. He looked just like the griffin carved over the door of the church. He was just as big and just as scary.

One day a bird told the Griffin about all the carvings on the church. That interested the Griffin. He had no idea what he looked like. Of course, there were no mirrors in the wild woods where he lived. And there were no other griffins for him to look at. He was the last one left in the whole world.

The Griffin decided he would go to see the carvings. So he left the wild woods and flew toward the old town. It took him a long time to get there. On the way, he flew over many towns, but he never landed. And that was just as well for the people who lived in those towns. Just seeing him fly over was enough to scare them.

At last he landed just outside the old town. By then it was growing dark, and his big wings were tired. He had not had to fly that far for many, many years. The Griffin decided to spend the night in a grassy place by the side of a brook.

Some people in the town had seen him coming. The news spread very fast. Many of the people were scared almost to death. They locked themselves in their houses.

The Griffin was not happy about that. He called in a loud voice for someone to come visit him. But the more he called, the more frightened the people became. Then he saw a farmer walking home from his field. The Griffin asked him to stop and talk for a while. The farmer was scared, too. But he did not dare run away.

"What is the matter with all the people in your town?" the Griffin asked. "Is there no one brave enough to talk with me tonight?"

The farmer thought for a long time. Then he said, "I think the Minor Canon might come and talk with you."

"Who is he?" the griffin said.

"He is a priest at the church," the farmer said.

"Go call him then!" the Griffin said. "I want to see him."

The farmer turned and ran down the road to the church.

The Minor Canon was a very fine young man. Besides holding church services, he did many good deeds. He visited sick people, poor people, and people with other problems. He was kind to everyone in town. He even taught at a school for the naughty children in town. They were the ones who would not behave at other schools. Nobody wanted anything to do with them. The Minor Canon was always ready to help others. That was why the farmer thought he might be willing to talk to the Griffin.

The young priest had not heard about the Griffin. He was surprised when the farmer told him about the strange creature. He was scared, too.

"Me?" he said. "He has never heard of me before. Why should the Griffin want to see me?"

"Who knows?" the farmer said. He did not want to tell the Minor Canon that he had told the Griffin about him. "I think you should go there right away. The Griffin is very angry, and you had better not keep him waiting."

The poor Minor Canon turned pale. He would rather have had his hand cut off than meet a griffin. But he knew that it was his duty to go. So he headed off to the place where the Griffin was waiting.

When the Griffin saw the young man, he said, "Hello. I am glad to see that someone was brave enough to visit me."

The Minor Canon did not feel very brave right then.

"Does your town have a carving that looks like me?" asked the Griffin.

"Yes," said the young man. "It is over the door of our church."

"Good," said the Griffin. "Please take me to see it."

The young man thought fast. If the Griffin came to town, the people would be afraid. Some might even be scared to death! The Minor Canon needed time to get them used to the idea of such a creature.

"It is getting dark," the young man said. "You will not be able to see the carving very well. It will be better if you wait until morning."

"That will be fine with me," the Griffin said. "I can see you are a man of good sense. Until tomorrow I will get some rest here in this soft grass. I can also cool my tail in the brook. The tip of my tail gets red hot when I am angry or excited. Right now it is very warm."

Then he waved a paw at the young man. "Good-bye. I will see you in the morning."

The Minor Canon was glad to get away from there. When he got to his church, there was a crowd of people waiting outside. They wanted to know what the Griffin had said.

The Minor Canon told them the Griffin did not want to cause any trouble. "He only wants to see the carving over the church door."

You would think that would have made the people happy. It did not. They got angry at the Minor Canon. "You should not have told him to come here!" one person said.

"What could I do?" the young man said. "If I did not invite him, he might come anyway. And he might get angry. He could set the town on fire with his red-hot tail."

Still the people were not happy. Then some of the old men came up with an idea. They thought the young men of the town should go and kill the Griffin. But the young men thought that was not such a good idea.

One man thought they should destroy the carving. Then the Griffin would have no need to come to town. That sounded like a good idea to everyone. All the people ran home to get tools to break up the carving. But the Minor Canon was against that plan. He felt it would make the Griffin very angry. The Minor Canon was worried. He stood in front of the door all night to protect the carving.

Early next morning he went to get the Griffin. The young man walked back to town, and the Griffin flew just above him. When they got to the church, the Griffin landed. He sat in front of the door, staring at the carving.

For an hour or more he stayed there, never saying a word. First he tipped his head to one side, then to the other. Finally he spoke.

"That is a very nice carving," he said to the Minor Canon. "I am sure it looks

The Griffin and the Minor Canon   33

just like me. Look at that big head and that sharp beak. It really seems like a fine piece of work."

The Griffin stayed there for the rest of the morning. The Minor Canon stayed with him. He hoped the Griffin would fly away, but that did not happen. The Griffin stayed there until it was almost dark. By then the Minor Canon was very tired. After all, he had been up all night protecting the carving.

To be polite, he asked the Griffin if he wanted something to eat. But as soon as he said it, he wished he had not. He did not know what the Griffin liked to eat. But he did know that the Griffin was a scary looking creature. What if he wanted a dozen babies, or some other treat of that kind?

But the Minor Canon had no need to worry. "No, thank you," said the Griffin, "I am not hungry. I eat twice a year— once in the spring and once in the fall. I just ate last week. I won't eat again for half a year. But *you* should have something to eat, if you want. As for me, I think I will go back to my grassy place and rest again."

The next day the Griffin came back to the church. He stayed there all day, looking at the carving. The Minor Canon came out a few times to keep an eye on the Griffin. And each time the Minor Canon came out, the Griffin smiled. He seemed glad to see the young man.

The Minor Canon could not stay at the church all day. He had work to do. Nobody in town went to the church that day. But that night many people went to the Minor Canon's house. They wanted to know how long the Griffin would be staying.

"I think he will go soon," the Minor Canon said. But he was wrong.

The Griffin came back to the church day after day. He loved to look at the stone carving. And he also seemed to like the Minor Canon very much. The young man had to leave the church often. He visited the sick and the poor. He went to the school to teach. After a while, the Griffin began to follow him everywhere.

People started to think the Griffin would *never* leave their town. They became very upset. At first, most people hid in their houses and peeked out the windows. The very rich people had already moved to towns far away. But most other people could not afford to move. Finally, they had to come out of their houses and go to work. The people were surprised that the Griffin did not try to hurt them. After a while they stopped worrying about him so much.

The Griffin and the Minor Canon were becoming close friends. The Griffin was very old and wise. He told the Minor Canon much of what he had learned.

All went well for a while. But when summer was almost over, the people began to worry once more. It would soon be time for the Griffin to eat again!

"He will be very hungry," one man said. "I'm sure he will want to eat up our children. What can we do about it?"

No one could answer that question. Finally, the people decided to ask the Minor Canon what he thought. He was the person they always turned to when they had a problem. They waited to talk to him until a time when the Griffin was nowhere in sight.

Yet even though they needed the Minor Canon's help, they were not polite about getting it. "It is all your fault," a woman said to the young man. "*You* brought the Griffin here. Now you had better find a way to make him go away!"

An angry man said, "You should go away yourself! The Griffin spends most of his time with you. If you go, he will follow you."

That made the Minor Canon very sad. "Where will I go?" he said. "If I go to another town, the Griffin will cause trouble there."

"Then you must not go to another town," the man said. "You must go to the wild woods. The Griffin will follow you there and not bother us again."

That night the Minor Canon thought it over. He decided that the people were right. He must go to the wild woods. That was the best way for him to get the Griffin out of town.

The next morning he set out on his trip. After a very long walk, he ended up deep in the wild woods. There were no people near him for miles and miles.

The Griffin missed the Minor Canon. After a few days he began to grow sad. He asked the people in town where the Minor Canon had gone.

No one dared to tell him. The fact that the young man was gone seemed to make the Griffin angry. The people did not want to make him angrier. So they told the Griffin they did not know where the young man went. Every day the Griffin grew sadder. He looked in all the places where the Minor Canon used to go. Of course, he did not find him.

One day the Griffin looked in the schoolhouse. None of the naughty children were there! They had stopped coming to school after the Minor Canon left town. That made the Griffin even sadder. He knew how much the Minor Canon cared about those children. He knew the young man wanted the naughty children to go to school. That was the only way they would ever learn to be good. So the Griffin decided that he would teach them himself.

When he rang the school bell, a few of the naughty children came out to see what was happening. When they saw the Griffin, they were afraid.

The Griffin told them to gather up all the other naughty children. "Tell them that I will be teaching school now," he said. "And if they do not come in 10 minutes—I will come and get them."

In seven minutes all the naughty children were there.

As bad as they were, they behaved very well that day. They did not dare to behave any other way.

When school was out that afternoon, the naughty children went home. The Griffin decided he would do some more of the Minor Canon's work. He went to visit the sick, just as the young priest used to do. Some of the sick got better as soon as he showed up at their houses. He made medicine for others. They soon got well, too. None of them wanted a doctor like the Griffin hanging around.

Time went by. It was now getting very close to fall. The people of the town began to grow more uneasy each day. They knew it was time for the Griffin to eat again. But what would he want for food? After he ate all their children, he might even want to eat the adults!

The people decided to invite the Griffin to a big dinner. They would roast a sheep. They would cook all kinds of meat and fish. They would give him any kind of food he wanted. Perhaps then he would be too full to eat them or their children.

By then they were sorry they had sent the Minor Canon away. He was the only one who was able to talk with the Griffin. But the Minor Canon was gone. So they sent an old man to tell the Griffin about the dinner they had planned.

The Griffin was not interested in the dinner. He told the old man he wanted nothing to do with the people of the town. "Those people are mean and selfish," he said. "I would not want to eat any meals that they cooked. And I *certainly* would not want to eat the people or their children. They are all cowards. The only one I could *think* of eating would be the Minor Canon. He was brave and good. He would have made a nice meal."

"Oh," said the old man. "We should not have sent him away to the wild woods."

"What!" cried the Griffin. "What do you mean? What in the world are you talking about?"

The old man told the Griffin why they had sent the Minor Canon away. That made the Griffin very angry. He flew in circles over the town, beating his wings. He got so angry his tail grew red hot. Finally he went to his grassy place. When he put his tail in the brook, it turned the water to steam!

This scared all the people. Most of them blamed the old man. One woman said to him, "See what you have done! The Griffin might have gone off forever, looking for the Minor Canon. Then all our troubles would be done with. Now that you have told him the truth, he will stay. He will cause all kinds of trouble!"

That same day, the Griffin came back to town. He rang the school bell. All the people knew what that meant. He wanted them all together so he could talk to them. The Griffin waited until they were all at the school before he spoke. Then he said, "I do not think much of any of you. I knew you were not brave. But I did not realize just how mean and selfish you all are.

"You have treated the Minor Canon very badly. He worked very hard to help all of you. And what did he get for it? You sent him away to the woods, just to save yourselves. You did not care what happened to him. All you thought about was how he could help you."

The Griffin's tail was getting redder and redder as he spoke. "I like that young man. Now I am going to find him and send him back here. This time you had better treat him right."

The people did not dare to say anything.

"There are only two good things about this town," the Griffin said. "One of them is the Minor Canon. The other is the carving of me. When I leave, I am taking that with me. Now all of you go home! I do not want to see your faces!"

The people were more than happy to get away from the Griffin. His tail looked so hot, they thought it might set the whole town on fire.

The next day the Griffin came to town again. He went to the church and tore the stone griffin from the wall. Then he flew away, carrying it in his paws. Soon he was back in his cave in the wild woods. There he stuck the carving over the cave door. Finally he went to look for the Minor Canon.

For hours the Griffin flew about, looking everywhere. At last he found him. The young man lay under a tree.

He looked very tired, hungry, and sick. Quickly, the Griffin picked him up and brought him back to the cave for a rest. The Griffin made medicine and soup while the young man slept. When he woke up, the Griffin took care of him. It worked wonders. Soon the Minor Canon was feeling much better.

The Griffin was very happy to see that his medicine had worked. It was good to see his friend feeling healthy. "You know," the Griffin told the Minor Canon, "I like you very much."

"Thank you," the young man said, "I am glad to hear it."

"You might not be glad if you knew the whole story," the Griffin said. "But never mind that now. I am angry at the people in your town. They treated you unfairly. But all that is over with. From now on they are going to treat you very well indeed. So lie down and rest some more. Then I will take you back to town."

A troubled look came over the young man's face.

"You do not have to worry," the Griffin said. "I will not be staying there for long."

He pointed to the carving that was now above the door to his cave. "I have this carving now, so I do not need to stay in your town. The fact is, I do not ever again want to see the people who live there."

The Minor Canon was happy that the Griffin would not cause trouble. He dropped back into a sound sleep. While he was asleep, the Griffin carried him back to town. He set him down next to the school. Then he flew back to his cave in the wild woods.

When the people saw the Minor Canon, they were very polite. They treated him well from that day on. They stopped being so selfish, too. They made him the head of the church and also the mayor of the town.

The parents in town also began to take better care of their children. They taught them how to be good. The Minor Canon no longer had to run a school for naughty children.

And slowly, the grown people began to behave as well as their children. At first they did good things because they were afraid of the Griffin. Then most of them got in the *habit* of doing good things. They became good because they *wanted* to be good.

The Griffin never came back to the town. When at last it came time for his meal, he did not eat. If he could not have the Minor Canon, he did not care for anyone else. And then one day he lay down in front of his cave and looked up at the stone griffin. There he stayed, without moving. After a few weeks he died. No doubt it was a good thing that the people in town did not know that.

If you ever visit that town, you can still see the little stone griffins on the church walls. But the large griffin that was over the church door is gone.

The Widow's Cruise

Have you ever had to "take a dose of your own medicine"? In this amusing story, a teller of tall tales meets his match. How could he have guessed that Mrs. Ducket had seen his kind before?

"THE WHALE HIT SO HARD HE ENDED UP WITH HIS HEAD INSIDE THE SHIP!"

The Widow's Cruise

Mrs. Ducket lived in a small town by the sea. She was born there, and had lived there all her 40 years. She was tall and thin, and active in both mind and body.

She was a widow—her husband had died at sea a few years earlier. She missed him but was quite able to take care of herself. Every day at 6:00 she got up and set to work. She cooked breakfast, milked the cow, and cleaned the house. Later she worked in her garden. In the afternoon she often knitted and sewed.

Mrs. Ducket liked to visit with her neighbors. She also liked to read—but not just any books. She liked true stories that had real people in them.

The widow shared her house by the sea with another woman named Dorcas Networthy. Dorcas was the widow's age, but the two women were quite different. Dorcas was short and plump. She tried to do everything the widow did, but she never was able to. Somehow she just didn't have the energy that the lively widow had.

One afternoon both women were sitting on the front porch sewing. Suddenly Dorcas looked up from her needle work. "Mercy on me!" she said. She pointed toward the road that ran by the house. A horse-drawn wagon was coming their way. There were four men riding in the wagon.

"Who do you think they are?" Dorcas asked the widow. "They don't seem to know how to drive that wagon. They keep going from one side of the road to the other."

Mrs. Ducket looked up from her needle. "It's easy to see that they are sailors," she said. "Sailors always drive a wagon that way. That is how they sail ships—they follow the wind from one side to the other."

"Your husband didn't like the sea, did he?" Dorcas said.

"No, he didn't," Mrs. Ducket said—for about the 300th time. For some reason, Dorcas was always asking that question. "My husband hated the sea," Mrs. Ducket went on. "He was drowned in the sea because he trusted some sailors. That is something I never did, and something I never will do!"

Dorcas pointed again. "Look," she said, "they have stopped their wagon. I think they plan to pay us a visit."

She was right. The men got out of the wagon and came up the path to the porch. The man who had been driving the wagon looked like the oldest. He had white hair and a little white beard. "Is this Mrs. Ducket's house?" he asked.

"That's my name," Mrs. Ducket said.

The old man spoke again. "I am Captain Bird," he said. "I was told that my mates and I might get a meal here. We have a long ride ahead of us and we are very hungry."

"You can get a meal here," the widow said. "It will cost you one dollar for each man."

The four men looked at each other, nodding and smiling. "That seems fair to us," the old man said to the widow.

"Fine," she said. "Come this way." Then she and Dorcas went into the house with the four sailors following them.

Mrs. Ducket and Dorcas joined the four men at the table. It was a good meal, and the sailors all seemed happy with it. When they were finished, Captain Bird spoke up again. "That was just right," he said to the widow. "Before we go, I would like to let the horse rest a little more.

Do you mind if we sit on your porch and smoke our pipes?"

"Not at all," said the widow. "I don't allow tobacco inside the house. But it is quite all right to smoke on the porch."

The men went out to the porch and sat down on the benches.

"Shall we wash the dishes now?" Dorcas asked the widow.

"That job will wait until the men are gone," Mrs. Ducket said. "Now I think we should take chairs out to the porch and join them. When sailors smoke their pipes, they often tell interesting stories." So the widow and Dorcas joined the sailors.

When Captain Bird had lighted his pipe, the widow spoke to him. "You must have seen many strange things in your years at sea," she said.

A smile came to his face. "We all have stories to tell," he said. "Would you like to hear some?"

"We would be happy to hear them—if they are true," the widow said.

"There isn't a thing that happened to us that isn't true," Captain Bird said. "In fact, let me tell you a true story about what happened to me once."

"Please do," Mrs. Ducket said. "I am sure we would like to hear your story."

"Yes," Dorcas said, "I am sure it will be very interesting."

Captain Bird took a deep puff on his pipe. Then he blew out a big cloud of smoke and began his story. "Once when I was sailing on a ship, a whale ran into us. He crashed the ship from behind. The whale hit so hard he ended up with his head inside the ship. The rest of him was sticking out the back.

"Water came pouring into the ship. At first we were afraid we would sink. We started to get our small boats ready. We thought for sure we would have to leave our ship."

"And did you?" Dorcas said.

"No, not at all," Captain Bird said. "The whale blew the water out his spout as fast as it poured in. It happened that there was a hole in the deck above his head. That old whale blew the water straight up through the hole and into the sea!"

"My, that was lucky for you," said Dorcas.

"Yes it was," Captain Bird said. "And all the while the whale was working his tail. It moved just like a propeller in the water. In two days' time, he had pushed us safely to land."

"My, my!" said Dorcas.

"I don't think anything stranger ever happened at sea," said Captain Bird.

"No," said Mrs. Ducket, "I don't believe anything ever did."

Then one of the other sailors took his pipe from his mouth. "Something very strange happened to me once," he said.

"Tell us, please," Dorcas said.

"Well," the sailor said, "it happened during a heavy fog. We had a very fast ship with two engines. As we were moving through the fog, we ran right into an island. All of us thought the ship would break apart. But that didn't happen. We were going so fast, we tipped the island upside-down. It is still that way today. When people sail over that spot, they can look down and see the roots of trees and cellars of houses."

"My, my!" Dorcas said, shaking her head.

"That reminds me of a trip I took once," another of the men said. "That time I was on an obelisk ship."

"Obelisk ship?" said Dorcas.

"Yes," the man said, "a ship that carries obelisks—those tall monuments that come to a point. They look like giant, fat needles made out of stone. In fact there is one in New York City. They call it Cleopatra's Needle. Have you seen it?"

Dorcas shook her head.

Mrs. Ducket said, "I have never been to New York City, but I have read about Cleopatra's Needle."

"Well, then," said the sailor, "you know what I am talking about."

Dorcas and Mrs. Ducket both nodded.

The sailor went on. "We were carrying an obelisk from Egypt to New York City. It was a really big one. To get it on board we had to cut a hole in the back of the ship. We slid that big stone needle in point first. Then we repaired the hole we had cut.

"As we sailed along, we came to a sand bar. We were going too fast to turn out of the way. Any other time we would have sailed right over the bar. But that obelisk was very heavy. We felt sure the ship would get stuck. When we hit the bar, our ship stopped dead. But that obelisk slid forward. It went so fast, it shot right out the front of the ship."

"Oh, my!" Dorcas said.

The sailor puffed his pipe and went on with his story. "That obelisk shot right over the sand bar and into deep water. Its heavy back end landed first. The pointed end was sticking up about five feet above the water. There was no way we could get that thing back on the ship. It was just too heavy. To tell the truth, I think it is still sticking up in the water to this day."

Dorcas shook her head from side to side in wonder.

Just then another of the sailors spoke up. "The strangest thing that ever happened to me had to do with a shark. We were sailing up near the North Pole. All around us were big pieces of floating ice—icebergs, they are called. Some of them were ten times as big as this house. And that was just the part you could see above water!"

"Oh," Dorcas said, opening her mouth wide.

"Well," the sailor said, "the ice on some of them was as clear as glass. And inside one of those clear icebergs we could see a shark. It was a big one—about 14 feet long. The captain of the ship wanted to get him out.

"Just then I saw the shark wink its eye. I told the captain, but he didn't believe me. He said if the shark was frozen in ice, it had to be dead. He forgot that sharks are different from other animals. They have cold blood, you know. They don't need much heat."

Dorcas didn't know that. She opened her mouth wide again and shook her head in wonder.

"Well," the sailor went on, "the captain cut the shark free. He took an ax and chopped away the ice. As soon as he did, the shark jumped into our boat."

"What a happy fish he must have been!" said Dorcas.

"Yes," the sailor said. "He was a happy enough fish. But we didn't have a very happy captain. You see, that fish had been in the ice for many years. It had not had a bit to eat in all that time. It was really hungry—as the poor captain found out, to his sorrow."

"You sailors really see some strange things," Mrs. Ducket said. "The strangest thing about them is that they are true."

"Yes," said Dorcas, "it *is* strange that all these stories are true."

"I, too, have a sea story to tell," said Mrs. Ducket. "Would you men like to hear it?"

Captain Bird looked up, a little surprised. "Why, yes, Mrs. Ducket," he said, "we would love to hear it."

The three other sailors all nodded.

"It happened a long time ago," Mrs. Ducket said, "when my husband was away. My sister lived across the bay from me then. Her husband was a fisherman who sometimes fished at night. She always put an oil lamp in her window so he could see his way home.

"One morning she sent a boy to me with a message. Her note said she was out of oil and wanted me to send her some. The boy was supposed to bring it back to her. But by the time I got a gallon can of oil ready, the boy had left on another errand. He never came back.

"When it started to get dark, I got worried. I decided to take the oil to her myself. If she couldn't light the lamp, her husband might get lost at sea. So I took the gallon of oil and went down to my husband's boat. I untied it and started across the water. When I was about a half mile away from shore—"

"Mrs. Ducket," Captain Bird said, "were you rowing the boat or sailing it?"

Mrs. Ducket gave the captain a strange look. "No," she said, "I wasn't doing either one. I forgot to bring the oars. But that didn't matter—I didn't know how to use them. And I didn't sail either, because I didn't know how."

"Then how did you—" Captain Bird started to say.

"I used only the rudder," Mrs. Ducket said. "I just turned the handle and that made the boat go."

"But Mrs. Ducket!" Captain Bird said.

"Well, that is the way I did it," she said. "When I was a half mile from shore, a big storm came up. The waves were bigger than houses. The sky was filled with thunder and lightning. I held tight to the rudder handle so that I wouldn't fall into the water.

"Then I remembered the oil. I took about a cup of it and poured it on the water. In three seconds or so, it went right to work. That oil made the water all around the boat as smooth as glass.

"I decided to rest while I had the chance. The big waves were jumping all around me. Sometimes the waves met and blocked out the sky. Even the water in the bottom of the bay was rough. There was a big crack in the boat and I could look down and see—"

"Mrs. Ducket!" Captain Bird said once more. The three other sailors all shook their heads from side to side.

"I could see big sharks down there," the widow went on. "If I fell in, I knew they might eat me up in a minute. So I began to turn the handle of the rudder again. I wanted to get out of there fast.

"Soon I hit more big waves. I had to pour more oil on the water until it was smooth. I kept that up for a while, but then I started thinking. By the time I got to my sister's house, I would be out of oil. What would be the point of going there?"

The four sailors all looked at each other once again. Their mouths were hanging open.

"Then all of a sudden, the oil can tipped over. All the oil spilled onto the deck of the boat! There was a lot of dust there, and it soaked up the oil. My heart was beating fast. I looked through the crack and saw the bottom of the bay. Lucky for me, I had come to a sandy part, just like a beach. I decided I would run along the sand until I got to shore.

"I filled the oil can with air. Then I tore out some boards to make the crack in the boat bigger. When it was wide enough, I started to climb down through it. And then I saw a big horrible turtle! I wasn't afraid of sharks—but turtles have always filled me with fear. There was no way I would get near a turtle!"

Captain Bird's face looked like it was made of stone. "And what did you do then?" he quietly asked Mrs. Ducket.

"I used electricity," she said. "Now please don't stare at me like that. That is just what I used. Have you ever rubbed your feet on a rug and got charged up with electricity? When you touch someone with the tip of your finger, they feel a shock. Well, I decided to get filled with electricity. I stood on one of the seats, which was dry. I rubbed my feet back and forth for a while. Soon I was just *filled* with electricity. Then I jumped over the side and swam to shore. I was so filled with electricity I couldn't sink."

Captain Bird stood up and reached into his pocket. "Mrs. Ducket," he said, "we want to pay you for the meals. And," he added, "for the entertainment."

"The meals are one dollar for each," she said. "The rest is free."

Each of the sailors handed Mrs. Ducket a dollar. A minute later they were in their wagon and ready to move off.

Before they started, Captain Bird got off the wagon and came back to the house. "Mrs. Ducket," he said, "I have a question for you. You never told us what happened to your sister's husband. If your sister had no oil, she couldn't light the lamp for him."

"The storm pushed him to land," Mrs. Ducket said. "And the next day I told him the story I told you. Then he went home and told his wife. When she heard it, she left him for good. And it served him right, too."

"Thank you, Mrs. Ducket," Captain Bird said. He turned and went back to the wagon. Then he and his sailor friends continued on their way.

When they were gone, Mrs. Ducket turned to Dorcas. "Not a one of their stories was true. Think of it!" she said. "They dared to tell me such tales in my own house."

"In your own house!" Dorcas said.

Mrs. Ducket took the four dollars from her pocket and looked at them. "Well," she said, "I think we can say we got even with them."

"Yes," said Dorcas, "we got even."

A Piece of Red Calico

Have you ever agreed to do a "little job" that turned out to be a big one? In this story a helpful husband takes on more than he can handle.

SHE LOOKED AT THE CALICO AND SAID, "IT DOESN'T MATCH THE PIECE I GAVE YOU."

A Piece of Red Calico

One morning, my wife handed me a little piece of red calico. She asked if I could pick up two yards of matching fabric. I told her that it would be no trouble at all. I put the sample in my pocket and took the train to my job in the city.

At lunch time, I stopped in at a large dry goods store. I asked the floor walker where the red calico was. "This way, sir," he said, leading me through the store. "Miss Stone, show this gentleman some red calico."

"What shade do you want?" she asked.

I showed her the piece my wife had given me. She took down a big roll of the red cotton cloth.

"Why, that isn't the same shade!" said I.

"No, not exactly," said she. "But it is prettier than your sample."

"That may be true," said I. "But, you see, I want to match this piece."

The clerk took down another roll.

"That's just the shade," said she.

"Yes," I said, "but it is striped."

"Stripes are very popular," she said. "Striped calico is being worn more than anything else."

"Yes, but this material isn't to be worn. It's for furniture, I think. Anyway, I want plain red."

"Well, I don't think you can find plain red unless you get Turkey red."

"What is Turkey red?" I asked.

"Turkey red is perfectly plain in calicoes," she answered.

"Well, let me see some."

"We haven't any Turkey red calico left," she said. "But we have some very nice plain calicoes in other colors."

"I don't want another color. I want stuff to match this."

"It's hard to match cheap calico like that," she said. And so I left her.

Next I went to a store a few doors up the street. I asked the floor walker, "Do you have any calico like this?"

"Yes, sir. Third counter to the right."

I went to the third counter to the right. I showed my sample to the salesman, who looked at both sides of it. Then he said, "We don't have any of this."

"I was told you did."

"We used to—but we're out of it now. You'll find material like this at an upholstery shop."

I went to a nearby upholstery shop. "Do you have any stuff like this?" I asked.

"No, we don't. Is it for furniture?"

"Yes," I said.

"Then Turkey red is what you want."

"Is Turkey red just like this?" I asked.

"No. It's much better."

"That makes no difference to me," I said. "I want something just like this."

"But that kind of calico isn't used for furniture."

"I should think people could use anything they wanted for furniture," I said.

"They can—but they don't," he said, quite calmly. "They don't use a red like that. They use Turkey red."

I said no more, but simply left. The next place I visited was a very large dry goods store. I asked the first floor walker I saw if they had red calico like my sample.

"On the second floor," he said.

I went up to the second floor. There I asked another floor walker, "Where will I find red calico?"

"In the far room to the left. Over there." He pointed to a far corner. I walked through the crowds of shoppers, floor walkers, and sales clerks. When I got to the far room to the left, I showed my sample. "Calicoes are downstairs," said the salesperson.

"They told me calico was up here," I said.

"Not this *plain* calico. *Plain* calico is downstairs at the back of the store."

I went downstairs to the back of the store. "Where will I find red calico like this?" I asked.

A salesman took my sample and looked at it. "We don't have this shade in that quality of fabric," he said.

"Well, have you got it in any quality of fabric?" I asked.

"Yes, finer quality." And with that he showed me some.

"That's not just the right shade," I said.

"No. It's finer and the color's better."

"But I want it to match this," I said.

"I thought you didn't care so much about the match," said the salesman. "You said you didn't care about the quality. You know you can't match fabric unless you match both quality *and* color. If you want that quality in red, you should get Turkey red."

I did not feel like answering him. I said, "Then you have nothing to match this?"

"No, sir. But they might have it in the upholstery department. Go up to the sixth floor."

So I got in the elevator and went up to the sixth floor. "Do you have any red stuff like this?" I asked a saleswoman.

"Try the upholstery department—other end of this floor."

I went to the other end of the floor. "I want red calico," I said to a floor walker.

"For furniture?" he asked.

"Yes," said I.

"Fourth counter to the left."

I went to the fourth counter to the left and showed my sample. The salesperson looked at it and said, "This would be on the first floor—calico department."

I turned on my heel, went down in the elevator, and left the store. I was quite sick of red calico. But I decided to make one more try. My wife had bought the red calico not too long before. There must be some to be had somewhere. I should have asked her where she got it. But it seemed such a simple thing at the time. Surely, red calico could be bought anywhere.

I went into another large dry goods store. As I entered the door, a strange feeling came over me. I did not want to take out that piece of red calico. If I had had any other kind of fabric with me, I would have asked if they could match that. But I didn't even have a pen wiper. So I walked up to a young woman and showed her my sample. Then I asked the usual question.

"Back room, the counter on the left," she said.

I went there. "Do you have any red calico like this?" I asked the saleswoman.

"No, sir," she said. "But we have it in Turkey red."

Turkey red again! I gave up.

"All right," I said, "give me Turkey red."

"How much, sir?" she asked.

"I don't know—say five yards."

She gave me a strange look as she measured out five yards of Turkey red calico. After that she knocked on the counter and called out "Cash!" A young girl, with yellow hair in two long braids, came up. The sales clerk wrote down the number of yards, the name of the goods, and her own number. Then she wrote the amount of money I handed her. It looked as if she wrote a few other things, too. She probably wrote the color of my eyes and the way the wind was blowing. She put all this information on a slip of paper.

After that, she copied this information into a little book. Then she gave the paper, the money, and the Turkey red cloth to the yellow-haired girl. This young person copied the slip into a little book that *she* carried. Then she went away with the calico, the paper slip, and the money.

After a very long time, the girl came back. She had my change and the package of Turkey red calico.

When I got home that evening, I gave the calico to my wife. She looked at it and said, "It doesn't match the piece I gave you!"

"Match it!" I cried. "Oh, no! It doesn't match it. You didn't want to match it. You were mistaken. What you wanted was Turkey red—third counter to the left. I mean, Turkey red is what they use."

My wife looked at me in surprise, and then I told her all about my troubles.

"Well," said she, "this Turkey red is much prettier than what I had. I wish I had thought of Turkey red before."

"I wish from the bottom of my heart that you had," said I.

Thinking About the Stories

The Lady or the Tiger?

1. What is the title of this story? Can you think of another good title?

2. Who is the main character in this story? Who are one or two of the minor characters? Describe each of these characters in one or two sentences.

3. All the events in a story are arranged in a certain order, or sequence. Tell about one event from the beginning of this story, one from the middle, and one from the end. How are these events related?

The Griffin and the Minor Canon

1. Which character in this story do you most admire? Why? Which character do you like the least?

2. Story ideas come from many sources. Do you think this story is drawn more from the author's imagination or from

real-life experience? What clues in "About the Author" might support your opinion?

3. An author builds the plot around the conflict in a story. In this story, what forces or characters are struggling against each other? How is the conflict finally resolved?

The Widow's Cruise

1. Good writing always has an effect on the reader. How did you feel when you finished reading this story? Were you surprised, horrified, amused, sad, touched, or inspired? What elements in the story made you feel that way?

2. What period of time is covered in this story—an hour, a week, several years? What role, if any, does time play in the story?

3. Compare and contrast at least two characters in this story. In what ways are they alike? In what ways are they different?

A Piece of Red Calico

1. All stories fit into one or more categories. Is this story serious or funny? Would you call it an adventure, a love story, or a mystery? Is it a character study? Or is it simply a picture the author has painted of a certain time and place? Explain your thinking.

2. The plot is the series of events that takes place in a story. Usually, story events are linked in some way. Can you name an event in this story that was the cause of a later event?

3. Is there a character in this story who makes you think of yourself or someone you know? What did the character say or do to make you think that?